dedicated to caroline

you believed in this book before i did
thank you

copyright

copyright © lee mawdsley 2024

this work is protected by copyright. except
for any use permitted under the copyright act
1968, no part of it may be reproduced, copied,
scanned, stored in a retrieval system, recorded, or
transmitted in any form or by any means without
the prior written permission of the author.

isbn: 978-1-7636226-0-9

thank you

mum
caro
nil
mel
ash
kerry
michelle
kim

your support, memories, time and
encouragement, have allowed me to grow and
find my way. this collection would never have
been possible, without you all.

trigger warning
this book contains content
about suicide

my love
was like
a sentence

it needed
an end

hold the dark

inside anxiety

you can't see the tears
they drown me within
filling my empty heart

you can't see my frown
i hide it under my smile
avoiding the questions that follow

you can't see my rage
it sits inside and eats at me
leaving me lighter as the day ends

you might see the sunrise
or maybe the sunset
yet you don't see the dark clouds
tucked away
deep in my chest

the leaves burn now
blended orange & red bring change
everything and everyone is different
there is no going back to what was
or wondering what could have been

time will not freeze or wait for you to catch up
people will continue to go about their day
and you will join them
masking the uneasy feeling you hold inside

you come to realise
nothing will ever be the same
there are no leaves left to burn
or seasons to bring change
everything is gone and different now

a cup of tea will always go cold
and there will never be enough layers
to hold warmth

you will not allow tears to fall
or the inside of your anger
to break through

so you push aside the truth

nothing you do will change the fact
that the ones you have known
are now distant echoes
forever touching the steps you take
without them

distant echoes

little white pill

take me into your darkness
show me
how it is supposed to feel

swallow me
or me you

let me give myself to you
like when i was a boy
lying in the sun

i'll close my mind
surrender my thoughts
my thoughts to your warmth

surrender to you
little white pill

one night
is all i ask
just one night
i'm yours

scattered thoughts
surrounded by
broken glass
lifting
floating in reverse
from the ground
up, back, together
connecting
to the place they once were
forming that security
that hold
that bottle
full, exhausted
overflowing with
unscattered thoughts
ready to explode

bottled up

timeless tears

is this the end?

the place
where love dies

where waves
no longer break

where flowers
no longer bloom

a grave yard
full of beautiful memories

a shoreline
no longer in sight

i am drowning
unable to breathe
through timeless tears

you absorb my anger
take my pain
i force it upon you

smashing you multiple times
over and over
you take my beating

i do not breathe

my lungs suffocating
as exhaustion takes over

i do not cry or slow
i do not stop
or give in to you

i run harder
faster

i do not look back

don't look back

no return

i hear your name
in the distance
like an echo
amongst mountains

i have no time
to reach you
to find you
to open my arms to you

within the corners of my mind
i struggle to find the light
i struggle to find you

the echo fades
and all that is left
is the view
above the treeline

it's a cycle

wet paint
that's how i see you
falling through my finger tips

you drip your pathetic existence
all over me

leaving fragments
you stain and tarnish all surfaces

you're a creep
your eyes appear over the shadows of things

filling the empty
with even more darkness

a suffocating grasp
you hold firm
and that's how i know
i'll never learn

push-pull

i walk along a cliff
you walk along a cliff
two unknowns

connections are formed
grafted
lives are intertwined
hands are held

we walk along a cliff
waves smashing against rock
unsteady, unknowns

i push
i am unaware
my mind hasn't felt
this intense, this rush

it fits so perfectly
like hand and glove

you almost fall
you feel my push
i catch you, hold you
take care of you
i do not understand
the pain in which i cause

you push
i almost fall
i reach out
you take my hand

you're scared
where will you go to?
if you let your feelings out
if your emotions are not safe

i am shocked
i blame myself
i should try harder
i will try harder
how could i have done this?
what am i doing wrong?

i share my thoughts
i care so deeply
unknowingly expressing
the opposite of what you need
unaware of how my emotions
make you run harder
faster

you push again
i almost fall
i reach out
you take my hand
you feel the weight
and it's harder to pull

you do pull though
and by pulling
you feel the emotion
that you're scared to face

you question everything
you go to your safe place
the one within you
and you think
"no one can help me"

you feel alone
you take care of yourself
like you've always done

and by doing so
you push again
so that the focus
is almost only, on yourself
that's how you feel safe

and all i want to do is hug you
reach out
pull you close
make you feel safe
loved
tell you you're not alone
you don't have to be
don't do it alone
because that's who i am
but that's not who you are

although somewhere inside
you may actually want that
it's the opposite of what i should do
because by doing that
i'm only pushing you more

so i don't push
i can't pull
i simply do nothing
because i'm now walking alone
on a cliff...
and i can no longer find you

the dark has a hold

it creeps along
the edges of things
through narrow alleyways
and shadowed graveyards

it has a movement
that folds silence within itself
an eerie presence
that evokes raised hairs
and heart rates

you wish to be any other place
but beside it
holding its hand

but here you are
and here it stays
ever gazing into your deep eyes
from its dark shadows

trapped, you hold still
feeling a deep pain within
as it wraps around your wrist
keeping time to itself

you'll never realise
you'll be its forever
until the day it's your last

i thought i was the clever
sneaky one
avoiding you at every turn

i was sure
i had washed my hands of you
leaving behind your sickness
for someone else to consume

you got me though
a debilitating presence
you infected me

you sucked away
the goodness
from my day

you're a disease
that really needs
to go away

unwanted

misunderstood

must i suffer lack of sleep
through endless thoughts
of tomorrow's unknowns?

is this a way
you'll make a move
to shift your cold piece?

to push away the loyal
and fulfill the void
finding the compliant
for your better tomorrow

do you save face?

i'm not like
your army of soldiers
who fall into line
leaving a sweetness
between your lips

i won't go into a darkness
or succumb
to the level in which you fall

your personal attacks
have not gone unnoticed

i may have sleep
taken from my time
these lonely hours
serve to educate

so if the time comes
tomorrow, or the day after
the hole you have dug
will require more than a shovel
to fill

burnt out

when the fire of life
is left without oxygen
it is sometimes hard to see
where the red gum
once was

left behind

fermented from the hours that passed
the old man seeked forgiveness
from his own heart

he sat afraid
unable to move beyond his thoughts

all of whom he had once known
would be a memory
he was forced
to leave behind

finding the night

she walked out
leaving bottles on the floor
no time for him

no cab sav will save them
no tonics over melted ice

you can't drink the night
once the day has begun

only the chill remains
lingering

it's a smoky ice
of empty ice trays

the new day brings tomorrow
no time to sleep it off

he grabs a new bottle
to find the night
once again

come join me

i escape into my darkness
to find the answers that haunt me

you can't see my scars
the feeling i wish to be held through

i am lost without you
and with you

it's an unhealthy balance
of burden

you break my walls
you break me

i build you up and all you do
is break me

i'm lost figuring out my anxiety
when i'm with you

it can't be one thing
and then another

is the complacent life
what you crave to hold onto?

the darkness only complicates
the complexities of what we already have

you don't follow me there
i'm alone

if only i could tell you
it was forever
without you realising
forever
wasn't enough

what's next?

into your bottle

it's not enough...
less

you wondered why
i left

i did, i do
still love you

the pain of maybe
hopefully

i held it
for you

it wasn't enough
and that's ok

time
will be enough

today hurts
tomorrow hurts
less

into your bottle
i go
let me sit alone in its corner
for no one else to find
but you

on my mind

sleep's on my mind
you find your way there

when you said
the silence of the night
leaves us with nothing but our thoughts
you were right

familiar moments are held for us
to wonder over and pull apart
to no good end

let me sleep so that you can lay to rest
nothing good comes from it

lack of sleep is all that follows
where the coffee of a new day
only helps bring me back to life
for a few good hours

night eventually comes though
and i find that sleep's on my mind
yet again

an empty letter

we don't talk anymore

i loved what we had

i tried to repair what i broke
was that a mistake?

i think about reaching out
again
and then again some more

but i won't
i already have

i can't undo what i've done
i can't change who i am
i don't want to
and yet
i do

when we talk
it is always the niceties

i'm supposed to let go
and i do
i always do

but then i don't

oceans gathered
consuming the very land she lay on

there were no more tears to cry

swept away was all she longed for

she drifted downwards
the cold would hug her
hold her

no more breaths to take
one hand out stretched

she met with darkness
a place of rest

find your rest

empty

i tore the flesh
from your heart

you might weep for years
although i think
knowing you

you won't even know
it's gone

we're not the same you and i
even if we look it

hiding under the surface
you move on

you're not frozen in time
circulating your thoughts
questioning your actions
the impact of your way

we're the opposites

holding on is all i've known
and letting go is all you care for

the words you use
the actions you take
they are not enough

show me more

more is what i long for

searching for more

choices

we wait for the sound
a soft
gradual build
from a rotating
distance tyre

as it approaches
we sometimes
step out

other times
we pause

we wait
for a split second

we wonder

life goes on
with or without us

to sit with

my eyes are heavy

a day without alcohol
no coffee for the taking

my mood longs for nothing
no one
masking a smile even hurts
i don't bother

i'm behind the door of another that's locked
suffering the self-inflicted indulgence
of a first world luxury
that we call a problem

hope is nowhere
not even on insta
where i doom scroll

until i'm finally
holding the uneasy hand
of my own

unavoidable pain
to sit with

comfort

not eating
is easy

the eating part
is hard

once it starts
it's hard to stop

the taste fills
the uneasy feelings
i'm avoiding

the sweetness touches my lips
salivating my mouth
helping me forget
even more

not even the feeling
of too much
is enough

i keep eating

not eating
is easy

i miss you sarah

your pauses
like time could wait
your chanel
now a shadow on the window sill
your runners
dusty and longing for pavement
your smile
the one that would welcome me home

when i close my eyes
my tears escape trying to find you

where's your favourite book gone?
the smell of those pages
the way you laughed and cried
how you laced one leg around mine
on our bed

i visit your side of the bed sometimes
it's cold

if i have to eat avocado on toast
again tomorrow
alone
i hope tomorrow never comes

i blame you for dying
me for living

i wonder where you are
what you are

all i know though
is where you are not
and that's
by my side

beside me

rain and pain

like waves crashing onto me
gaps between sets
me gasping for breath

like the ice in my gin
numbing my lips
as i sip
and my hands
as i hold it

like my tears
as my emotions get the better of me
the cold chill they create
as they run down my face

like the lead in my pencil
shaping my shadows
creating a darkness

like the storm in my stomach
tossing me this way and that
with an uncertain outcome
that will eventually pass

rain onto me...

let me brave
what i must face

the dancer

she touches the surface
her feet dancing
this way and that

a lightness
gracefulness
not even she is aware of

she moves and sways
bends and folds
connecting with the music

there is a beauty
reflected from within
built up over years
lessons upon lessons
pain, sweat, tears

a hardship only some
may ever witness
yet most don't

as the music continues
her beauty is all we see
an external moment
glimpsing into the internal

showing all that she is
and maybe even
all that she will ever be

is she open?

open she is not

with words to speak
thoughts to think
or moments to fill

she is not open

to open up
to find the struggle
to face yourself
to face your thoughts

now that's a thought

to look into the mirror
to reflect
to see whats on the other side
to sit with it

to sit with it

open she is not

the darker hours

sleep takes forever
thoughts make it worse
i push them down
they vomit up

i've turned over
counted sheep
it doesn't help

the pillows soft
sleep is coming
the thought wakes me

outside
a car passes
the roof cracks
no one's considerate

i fall asleep

i'll reattempt
the darker hours
tomorrow
yet again

old scars

revisiting
the scars you create
can be ugly

save me
from this space
these people

take my hand
forgive me
set me free

kill me
take my pain
touch me
let it be

say it's ok
tell me in time
let me hide
let me not

punish me
for have i not?

one tear
two
i can't count them all
i'm sorry
i'm sorry
i'm sorry
is true
now where to

too late is all i hear
from my mouth
to my ear

bury me
say it's ok
tell me it's over
take it away

punish me now
again and again
i'll take all the beating
even if there's no end

i am the judge
the jury
guilty i say

so hang me
a picture will do
display me for all
showcase the shame

i'll drown me
in alcohol
a place i can hide
again
and again
and again
until i die

cherry

i'll take you tonight
my sweet cherry
a comfort of sorts
so the darkness
may come early
so that restfulness
will find a home
amongst soft pillows
and fresh sheets

i lay still
forever

you hold the weight of my day
your long hug
left full

tomorrow's adventures
will come
so i'll take you tonight
my sweet cherry

tonight
is all i have

tonight
i'm yours

can you hear me?

i hide behind
the words i use
to express how much
you mean to me
neglecting
my voice
inside

i kissed your glass lips
for the final time

the bottle
lay empty

finally
an ending

when the end comes

what would you kill for?

i feel like i'm dying
it's a slow death
the unpleasant kind
each day you know it's coming
you just don't know when

i feel like i'm being taken
like a slow chemical change
on a microscopic level
and i can feel the subtleties

to everyone else
i'm the same

the worst part is not knowing
always guessing
reacting to my subtleties
which might be this or might be that

i feel like i'm dying

and maybe that's ok
maybe not having a tomorrow
is better

where the subtle pain
no longer lingers
and takes up a space
it calls home

i'll find my place to rest
without suffering
without the never ending stress

maybe dying isn't so bad
it might actually be
the better half of me
the half that would kill
for rest

there are times
you dim the light
hide away
close the door

it's sometimes the hardest
to ignore

to appreciate
what you have
when you search and long
for more

unable to hide

your feelings
remain

your resistance
relentless

hold the grey

hold the cork

my outer bark
holds within
the uncertainty

this is where
i am
the vulnerable

parts of me i share
others i do not

as trust is built
words
may lighten

thoughts
may soften
slowly allowing
bottles to float

a place i find
where the core aligns
with my true self

although
the difficult part
always being
the ones you choose
to hold the cork

future you

we all have histories
unchanged
set in stone

we all live in the present
choices
shaping our existence

we do not have a future
tomorrow
for it will never come

we only have now
moments
ever changing

we only have dreams
desires
pathways to the unknown

my beach

i feel your soft touch
on my feet
between my toes
as i walk with you
on you

i feel your chill
against my cheeks
as i stare out
into your depths
never ending

how open you seem
yet how guarded
and unknown you are

i could become lost
in you

as the night fades
and unfolds onto itself
as you lay still
nestled on your bed
softened by your pillow
do you question?

i hope one day
you see what i see
i hope one day
you let that someone in
and this time
you hold on

instead of resisting
pushing or hiding
and continuing what must be
an agonising
lonely cycle
of letting go
what could have been

do you question?

i gave you time

the sun sent warmth
into her cold
empty heart
filling it once again
with time

moments to ponder
and time

silence opens doors
letting in
the vulnerable

weight lifts
acceptance enters
doors close
once again

waiting
for silence

be silent

finding space

i see you in the sky
i wonder if you see what i see

shapes of clouds
patterns
a distance
a gap that no longer can be filled

the clouds break
separate
float off into opposite directions
like us
leaving an emptiness
a space
that is needed

the clouds might come again
yet there is only so much
we can take
the storm only seems to grow

we need to see the sun
to shine
we can't seem to shine together

moments pass
and then days
it starts to rain
i find shelter
you find shelter
we just can't find shelter together

and so we don't

your words calm me
make me feel safe

when you're close
i feel the same

my body relaxes
my chest no longer pulls
from the inside out

my mind opens up
to the space it once knew

the work is mine
a burden
you no longer deserve

because when it comes down to it
i need me
before i need you

i need me

letting go

i give it my all

i explored the road traveled
graveled
and not at all

at times
I feel an inflicted aching
and question
the choices of my making

letting go
brings so much aching

and although it's right
it's still not easy

it's still the hardest thing
to face
to do

the hardest path to walk
where the only way through
is letting go
of you

like the last
rose petal
gently floating
side to side
returning
to be grounded
once again
so that one day
it may return
grow
bloom
differently

reborn

more is less

when values
are out of alignment
change is coming

when i need you
you are not there
a hard truth to face

be grateful
you say
that isn't enough though
i want more

more means pain
for you
and for me

you don't want more
in fact
you gave less

try to see
what i see
it hurts to look
you don't look

i am unsure what i am
but i've always been grateful

i'm doing this for me
i am trying to live my best life
and i am taking away
the pressure
so you can live yours

i see no other way
you give me
no other option
maybe because
there is none

it's not the time
for silence though

does this mean
i am not grateful?

i feel so grateful
all i wanted was you
did you not feel that?

you keep saying
you can't give me
everything i need

the truth is
we can't give each other
the things we need

it hurts

i'm sorry i missed the chance
to see you one last time
to shake your firm hand
and hug your strong shoulder

our visits
though few and far between
were cherished

moments i've hung on to

you remind me of me
the drive
keeping busy
your determination

i feel honoured to carry that with me

thank you for all the laughs
the memories and good times
especially by the beach each year

it won't be the same
without you

when it's your time

what is love?

you are upset
angry
maybe you hate me

i do care though
which is why it has to be
this way

to continue
will only hurt more
prolong
the inevitable

i hope you see
one day
that this is love

that love
isn't always holding on
sometimes love
is letting go

time
spinning, twirling, tapping
forming from the ground up
solid roots
growing, grasping
holding on to fragments
of moments
forgotten or not
the unseen
unspoken
unknown
time

find your dry tears

the ocean
ran from your eyes today

i could feel
the depths of your pain

the hurt
shadowed your fragile mind

at a loss
occupied by consuming thoughts

you were used
unfairly taken advantage of

it was hard to hold back my anger
so i cried instead

you do deserve
so much more

take a step back
so you're able to step forward

there are better things
floating out at sea

for they will dry your tears
not create them

when i'm with you
time is forgotten
life is still
calm
it all feels right
for once

when i'm with you
your beauty radiates
beaming out to me
like sunrays through trees
connecting with me

when i'm with you
my eyes won't wonder
you flood my mind
leave me full of images
full of thoughts
full

when i'm with you
my happiness peaks
i feel the mountain
will go no higher
but you surprise me
and i climb some more

when i'm with you
i feel alive
moments become memories
thoughts become reality
a lifetime wouldn't be enough

when i'm with you
i feel happiness
so much warmth
and endless love

when im with you

when i'm with you

our time

i ran past the place we met

it brought back the moments
and memories of our time

such a good time

when i close my eyes
i can feel my cheek
against your hair
the warmth as i hugged you
and held you
for what seemed like
the first time
every time

we absorbed each other
in those moments
the burden of life
left weightless

i gave my heart to you
and you me

life is unpredictable
unforgiving

i guess that time
was our time

am i floating?

i have lifted back the layers
that keep me boxed within
each one holding the weight of the other

when i think about next steps
i no longer think about things
that once held me grounded

i'm floating
with endless options
and unfortunate feelings of excitement and dread

hoping that what's to come
will continue to shape the values and beliefs
i hold close to my authentic self

trying to find and navigate a new pathway
to an uncertain future
using skills and concepts
time has given me

look up

as the sun sets
the orange glow on the horizon
slowly parts for the day

how lost we are
hidden in our screens
searching for happiness
validation
beauty

hoping for things to change
for something better
bigger
brighter

do we crave more?

if so
more is what we receive
inside our phone
at least

abandoned

you think
i abandoned you

i understand
it's your worst fear

i tried to meet you
half way

i tried to meet you
all the way

i have answered
every message and always will

together or not
friends or not
i have never abandoned you

I feel
you have abandoned
yourself

triggers

the complexities of the past
disrupt the pathways of the present
contributing to the impact of the future

we do not know time
all we know
is how to survive
how to protect ourselves
from the pain
from the past

so we form beliefs
triggering us
through past memories
without realising
they are holding us down
holding us back

we are set in stone
ever fixed on ideas
of yesterday
unable to move forward
into today

if only we knew
that discomfort
was the answer
letting it be present
might allow it
to eventually pass

the stone
would start to crumble
even though
parts may still
hold weight

feeling discomfort
might allow us
to move freely
into a future
of possibilities

and then maybe
we might see
we are stronger
and more resilient
than we ever imagined
we ever could be

if the love i had for you
fit within a grain of sand

if i were dropped
on a deserted beach
for nobody to find

i would wait for you there

tides would come and go
the sun would rise and fall
ships would dock
the presence of others
would be felt

one day
like a washed up bottle
amongst the many
you may find me
yet again

and even though
i might be grey and old
slow and wise

you would still fill the crack
you had once left
in my heart

i'm a grain of sand

i miss you

it's not possible to say how or why
the moments just come and go
and the words just hold true

i don't think

i type and it's as if my thoughts
float onto the page
fall one after the other
like building blocks

i stack them higher and higher
underneath those three words
underneath…

i
miss
you

if only we could
condense the thoughts down
squish them into meaningful
bite size snacks
so that others could grasp
an understanding of what we have inside

maybe then
moving forward
wouldn't be the task
we once thought

maybe then
moving forward
wouldn't be a task at all
and instead
a walk to be remembered

many thoughts

mountain views

undiscovered
shadowed thoughts
hold us back
from mountain views

from peaks made of sweat
dripping in oceans vast
of sunsets rich
to valleys darkened and deep

we find riches untold
unexplored
of undiscovered beauties
where hidden pockets
have no seams

beyond the eyes
within our mindset
we shift our shadows
lighting a new way

pathways uncovered
untraveled
where fresh marks sink deep
ingrained within lush forests
long and wide

here we find that
growth follows
so stagnant minds
can lay to rest

so that rivers dry
can now flourish
and soften the soil
of steps taken

of progress
of beginning
finding and exploring
so that the meaning
can take shape

leaving behind
broken pieces
to be mended
on that journey
up ahead

time is all we have
and at the time
it's always enough

realisation

stepping into the light

we sometimes feel a deepness
a darkness
that hurts to hold on to

where past memories
cloud new ones
waiting to blossom

if timing where different
maybe too
would be
the alignment

you can't connect
with shadows

there is no future
in the dark

at the root

i've been placed in the bottom drawer
left with my thoughts to rest on
and reorganise

it's dark down here
so many things to sort
to fold away

it's cold down here
questioning everything
is ultimately
the only goal

i'll wait down here
alone and where i belong

but i'll hope down here
for a new day
a new dawn

it is and will be

ripples formed
from life's droplets
slowly finding
shallow shores

they fall so elegantly
a slow motion of sorts
where time holds value
between their gravity

you can grasp them
control a direction
but no matter what
you can't prevent
the important things
in those moments

future ripples
forever moving
and changing
must adapt
to grow

i checkout

the sun warms the side of me
that still holds thoughts of you
every time i visit a place we once knew

i sit wondering and overthinking

do you have thoughts of me
the pain i caused
the friendship i struggled to let go of

i notice an unspoken pain
on the random times i've seen you
every time you pass

to check in
would be to dishonour
your life and sadness i brought

so i checkout
leaving you walk on
back to your life
i now know nothing of

hoping i haven't stirred up
old memories
you'll possibly ponder
that same night

new days

he felt the unknown
set upon him

looking back
and lingering longer
he watched her

she reluctantly stepped away
turning to hide her pain
face her guilt

the deep rooted strength
she needed
was inside
she searched for it

knowing they would be ok
alone and separated
a sad
perfect fit

surrendering
left a bittersweet

a sour uneasy feeling
of lost love and relief

and as the year ended
where life's choices
were left to sit

the unknown
set upon her
and new days
upon him

don't let go

be the warmth
zip me up
on these cold and gloomy nights

wrap yourself around me
until i can't breathe a single breath
allow me to feel
once again

don't let go

thaw me out
smother me
end to end
and back again

i want you to hold that
hold me
trap me into your future
of unknowns
the place i want to be

misinformed

his body moves from the sidewalk to the steps
he travels downwards with speed and grace
over and under railings
through man made obstacles
he jumps and maneuvers

his strength a mechanical motion
racing
aiming towards his destination
as a shadow follows
trying to take hold

he approaches
trips and falls
reaching up with one hand
holding out the life for another

just in time

he completes his last task
right before malfunction
and saves his master
for the last time

there are many people
that fit within
the fabric we are sewn into
and then
there are many who do not

don't hold on
to a concept
of a soul mate

there are many

some
you let go of

others
you find a hold

searching

hidden pain

let the fire burn

let the embers find a place to settle

find the pain

believe the pain

don't trust your mind

sit there in silence

hold its hand

be still

life's lessons

yesterday
imprints time stamps
within our delicate minds

bodies of burden
unable to escape
meet the many years
of unrelenting stress

will they lose their hold
soften the moments
as we grow old?

or will we grow old
allowing moments
to hold?

old habits

like boats rocking
we were unable to find
our true centre

you are not to blame
it was not your fault

you held on to the past
which knew you so well

seeking comfort
in old habits

you craved the space
i had taken

aging oak

it ends
time

the last bottle
sinking sand
vanishing amongst the pages

waiting for the words
for the black ink to soak paper
to imprint

waiting

memories are for safe keep
stored away within an aging oak
lock and key
shared with love

connected
where trust is built
earned

so we wait

we wait
for time

a clear future

your future was clear
so i wrote mine
alone

i let the naked flame hold me
nobody will be watching

my growth continues to climb
all the walls i have rebuilt

all i see is the horizon now
the urge to move
towards the answers i long for

i leave you behind

the one i cherished
the one i cared so deeply for

the river at times runs from my eyes
into my aching heart

the tide does go out
and at times i do feel your absence

in the end

i'll no longer allow my hands to be tied to the content you feel
towards a life you no longer appreciated with me

and so you'll do you
and i'll do me

i'll do me

let go

i avoid the subject
skip the hour
i take the minutes
before i cower

each one i hold
and later find more
during the night
the glass i pour

i take the drink
it takes the hours
the days last long
and the sheets grow sour

my eyes find the pillow
it weeps for my rest
my phone finds my eyes
and the rest is

next
next
next

two days seem to pass
recovery is close
i'll find some time
after dinner and a note

the darkness does come
you're not by my side
the sheets lay bare
i cry

the next day i must
focus will come
sleep is important
like the moon and the sun

find me in dreams
8 hours i'll give
the darkness will love me
like the days as a kid

avoiding the screens
my mind seems to care
it's conditioned and longing
yet i opt for cold air

hours which pass
the minutes to me
allow me to find
the courage to be free

treeline

up above the treeline
i find my butterflies

it's where i take the stress
and give the warmth

the reason is not always clear
right then and there

seasons come and go
yet you remain

until one day you realise
a lifetime wasn't enough

life's path changes
forks out into rooted unknowns

we take different paths
you and i

we walk it alone
no longer hand in hand

unable to see
eye to eye

in hope that one day
we'll find the treeline
once again

i pave the way for success
as failure follows
racing towards a finish line
that i know
i will never see

hold the light

sunny day

pour onto me
let me take you
feel you
embrace you

let the warmth
go deep within my veins
unfold onto me
touch me

i will move
so you don't have to
or i will travel
and you can follow

stay
do not hide away
let me close my eyes
and focus on you
on this sunny day

i am not alone

the slowest of breaths...
i take

the calmest of thoughts...
i think

the warmest of touch...
i feel

your smell floods me...
i am still

your hands hold me...
safe i feel

your words soothe me...
it is real

i am not alone

where did i go?

there is a sad stillness
a calm
to my mind

i no longer feel
occupied

i am almost
me
again

how i have missed you
longing
to surface

fragile
although slowly hardening
to become solid once again

time may yet heal
the sadness in my heart

letting go
to move forward
to grow
becoming
the person i need to

finding
me

i find the souls of those
who seek to be found
amongst the dust of stars
they sing to me
like soft hums from a piano
as they float by
past the planets of tomorrow
reminding us about life
that all must move on
into a darkness
a black hole
to find the light once again
to find home

a lost soul

new connections

i felt drawn to you
a force pulling
or directing
my intuition

a feeling of warmth
rekindled passion
where two people
connect in such a way
that they burn as one

i wanted to absorb
every word
and every part
...of you

i am reminded of you daily
from the smallest of things
a floating leaf
the warmth of the sun on my back
waves breaking
the sand beneath my feet

i wonder where you are
how you are
and i hope
your life is fulfilled

i hope that
you
found your happy

find your happy

closure

my heart bleeds
it longs for you
for that deepness
that connection
two forces pulled
so strongly

when we kissed
i was lost within you
one touch
i would forget my way

we became one
in those moments
you and i
i miss those moments

i burn for you daily
even after
the candle goes out

how i hope
you are happy
unburdened
by my love

i do not contact you
not because i don't care
or my love for you has faded
you deserve to move on
from a decision i made

it will only prolong
any pain
i have caused

how i wish things were different
a time it could have been

how i wish
we could have grown old together
you and i

but i'm a dreamer
you are the realist
we are the opposite
maybe this is why
our connection
was strong

how i miss your kids
our friendship
the summer days
and nights
treasured memories
forever mine to keep

you were not bad for me
i do not regret our time
i found myself
that is all

i was lost when i met you
floating out at sea
searching for something
trying to find myself

you found me
and eventually
i found myself again

as i discovered my values
my needs
my boundaries
i burdened you

i asked for more
it was never the deal
i know

i say goodbye to you
every time i leave the beach
my favourite place
now also my saddest

as the sand leaves my feet
i weep for you
knowing i couldn't have you
the way i wanted

i realised
it wasn't fair on you
wasn't possible

you already gave me
all you could
it hurt so much
to let go

i couldn't give you
what you needed
in the end
without sacrificing
what i needed
and for that
i'm truly sorry

i apologise
if i didn't handle it well

forgive me

maybe one day
if the pain softens
or the clouds finally part
we might find a friendship
waiting to be rekindled

you opened up your heart
and i cherish that
i know that wasn't easy

i'm sorry if you regret
the time with me
telling me
your story

I do hope
you are now living
your best life

thank you for everything

goodbye

you

i open my eyes and see you
i see you

you are not forgotten
lost, unimportant
unable to surface

you are brave
be brave

you are strong
be strong

do not hide within
and push yourself
to the depths of your unknown

you may be understated
so reach out, up
one hand or two

you may see
finally
after all those years
what i see

you may see you

i sit and think
my thoughts
float between
the then
the now
the future

i am able to grasp
and reflect
build
and grow

i can see clearly
for once

i am able to
move
with my emotions
not against them

the darkness
has faded
the light creeps in
allowing
showing
the openness
of life
of love
of happiness

this feels
like the beginning
of a never ending

so i smile
at what could be
but also
at what is
and what was

because all moments
are memories
and all memories
are us

us

in its time

as winter ends
the trees no longer lay bare
small buds form
florets become visible
slowly inching their way forward
to generate
the growth that once was

they extend further
and further, until
peduncle elongation
right before
white petals
peak and bloom

how short a life, one is
a fleeting moment perhaps
the beauty
of impermanence

it shows that
there is but no time
now is all we have
we grow
as the cherry blossom
we hold on, live, change
and one day
we die
like a warrior in battle
the red flesh weeps from us
returning to the earth
once again

it is a celebration though
for the love of life
as life has its place
where moments
hold their beauty
and we realise
that everything
happens
in its time

during the winter
you warm me like the sun

through the dark nights
you keep the light on

when the heavy rain falls
you cover me

as raging thoughts visit
you guide me

you catch my tears
yet to fall

open my heart
to the unexpected

and allowed me
to lean on you

you never offer one hand
always two

you are the sun
and my moon

i do hope one day
i'll be able to support you

even if only half as much
as you do

support

see you there

my eyes weigh heavy
slowly bringing
peaceful darkness

into a world
of unknowns
i go

mixed amongst thoughts
within dreams
i rest

i will wait for you there

on a small wooden bench
over looking sand weeds
deep blue ocean
distant green mountains

i will see you there

this night
and the next
until the sun rises

bringing the warmth
of a new day
bringing the warmth
of you

it's all on the table

i feel loved by you
even though our time together
has been short

there is something naturally beautiful
about our connection

we see each other in a raw form
unshadowed by complexities

we simply place our complexities
on the table
and respect that

there is space between us
yet it grows mutually closer
each day

i slow my mind to be present
enjoying now
no matter what later holds

yet
i secretly hope
later holds you

be still

within a moment of patience
you're able to hold beauty

beauty is hidden
within moments

be still

accomplished

i cry out the happiness
i'm unable to hold inside

i've known pain
this is different

this is accomplished
self-inflicted pain
where giving up
is not an option

this is grueling pain
body and mind pain
this is
next level pain

stopping is absolutely necessary
and yet
you push beyond
and beyond some more

to reach an end
is to begin a journey

and so i cry out
again
and again
and again
until my body's sore

in search of the end
so i can struggle
some more

those words

words are crafted
from thoughtfulness
bringing together
the empathy
from you

from within you
i see
the beauty and kindness
a symphony
playing out
a masterpiece

you, i hear
a breathtaking moment
to hold on to
soak up
keep forever
within

those words and thoughts
expressed with love
in open arms
a hug

those words
moulding themselves
to me, for me
around me
to ponder
to question
to sit with

those words
to sit with

moments to hold
puddles to step through and not over
shoes to hang out to dry
next to his

a life that
until this very moment
was foreign

with a hand to hold
for all the new tomorrows
all the new forevers
and never ending nows

she would reach out
and he would take it

when you know

my life's purpose

a family is what you hold
in a life in which you value

your awareness is the space
you find before your step
just pause

you go easy and go hard
step forward and then step back
where limits are never reached
you crave beyond
and beyond some more

you find the love within
as you slowly realise
you are the foundation
nature will find the roots

happiness then follows
you are no longer a lost child
holding the hand of another

the space to let go
and meditate
is always now
it grounds the work
for the future
you may never see

you'll live in the moment
where the small things
are the meaningful

finding your health
learning new things
you search for the balance
where there is always a middle
before an end

you show your support
to the ones who deserve it
your time is precious
say no

you always listen
and love with meaning
take care of your mind
and fuel your body

there is no comfort zone
anymore

through your true authentic self
you realise your journey
is your peak

and even though
you'll never meet the end
you'll always understand
the purpose itself
is the living in life
and not the life you're living

what we miss

i notice
the sand rings around rocks
left behind by the tide as it makes its way out

i notice
my footprints and those of others
temporary time stamps of the past

i notice
the random coloured doggy bags
to be picked up on the return

i notice
the silence as i approach a bend
the wind has no home there

i notice
a couple looping their hands
threading each arm to form a hold

i notice
and wonder what else we miss

love

it is depth
continuous
growing layers
each one
strengthening
the next
it's more like memories
mixed with emotions, feelings, thoughts
it's everything over time
brought together
until the connections are so strong
that taking them away is painful
because you care so deeply
crave the closeness
it isn't just how you feel
it's also the small things
a look, a hug or a touch
openness, calmness
silence and all the in betweens
a comfortable presence
being prioritised

it isn't singular
it can't be

we dream

i've taken a journey
to find myself
like most

a path of navigation
through winding roads
and new experiences

i've read books
made memories
and spoken to wise ones

all in hope that one day
in a way that makes sense
i'll understand myself

and what i learnt was...

growth is never ending
memories guide us
time is an illusion

and so
we dream

the life she gave

her hand holds the life she gave
as she lays it down to rest each night
you feel the warmth of her letting go

the smell of pancakes engulf the kitchen
as she feeds the hungry mouths
who are idle around the table

as disaster spreads its wings
in a time where you feel not enough
she untwists the vines that bind you

you plant a seed together
in hope that the memory stays
and growth follows

time moves forward
the expectation and burden
released through discovered balance

until a time when her tide creeps in
showing you the hand that once held you
is drifting beyond a place of her unknown

as she sits looking outside
admiring the colours of the season
you bring her a dish she once made

the tree now shows the wrinkles of age
through weathered time
born from a place of love

you take her hand when she's lost
showing her the pathway back
if only for that moment

in the end her warmth fades
beside her bed you comfort her
as you lay her hand to rest
for the final time

i take two steps towards you
and wrap my arms
around your warmth

all that i am
falls and melts away
and i'm left

above the treeline

that place we long for

spend it wisely

sunday comes and sunday goes
it waits for no one

we tick boxes and meet deadlines
and do it all again
the next day

we seek freedom
through happiness
and reach goals
with friends we hold close

nothing could possibly be
more important

kept forever

you're on my mind
between sunflower meadows
and open blue skys

you peak through the sun rays
where the new pink ladies blossom
and the bees fly by

at times
it's hard to place
my head on my pillow
and forget those moments

i try
but you seem to fill the empty holes
that long for the love that we shared

and although i've moved on
towards new days
and new nights

the place you once held
will forever be ingrained
into the essence
of my mind

thank you

you opened my mind
i feel free

free to be myself
have space
and have time

time to question
to grow
time
to fill

thank you
for being open and honest
determined and strong
thoughtful

for sharing
trusting me
for your understanding
and for your warmth

thank you for caring
for listening
and not judging

for equality
balance
and for your flow

thank you for your passion
your desire
your emotions

for letting me hold the cork
to your bottle

you inspire me
through your style
your integrity
your resilience

thank you for
your empathy
your independence
it's a skill

you are so intelligent
hard working
and deserving
of a happy and fulfilling life

i appreciate you so much
and everything we share

i am forever grateful

with you
it feels like home

8am girl

you're on the beach
it's 8am

i have my coffee
you have your phone

i walk ahead
you walk ahead

on different days
it's the opposite

it almost feels
like i'm following you

i'm not

i make an effort to walk longer
when you turn
to prove a point to myself

as i walk back
some days you're in the water
other days you're not

i admire the way the sun falls on you
how water droplets sparkle on your skin

i lay on the beach to read
you take your dog home

your morning swim
is done

see you at
8am

silent strokes

silent strokes
soft hands
warmth
pressure

running hands
moving bodies
wet lips
intense heart beats

heavy breathing
silent bodies
closed eyes

warmth
silent strokes

they're off their leads
mingling and mangling
as wild as can be
free to roam the sand
the surf and sea
carefree
and yet
they are as tame
as me

wild things

memories for me

you're the woodgrain
lines carved
rings
the dints from time
knotted moments
held together
memories
to hold on to
memories
to keep

solid as a rock

you're my holey rock
not the religious type
the solid type you lean on
carved by the ocean
stood upon
unnoticed even
skimmed across water
kept in a pocket or two
well travelled

the hole's a symbol of wear and tear
buried and exposed
scars from a past well lived

on the sand
you wait
amongst the many

a place you can rest
until found

missed moments

the warmth
is on my back

waves meet kids
at the shoreline

a runner comes and goes
i long to join them

dog owners
toss sticks and call out commands

sand fleas
bother me

march flies
seem occupied elsewhere

seagulls cast shadows
on the surface of the water

i curl my toes into the sand
i connect with it

i close my eyes
i realise

i'm the only one
with a phone out

i long for your touch
to feel the cool warmth
from your hands
your body
to strip you down
naked
vulnerable
to glide my fingers
over yours
between yours
admiring the curves
beauty
the imperfections
that make you
you
that i crave
even more

i long to touch you
hug you
get lost
in you

your touch

make time

you don't have to hurry
she said
yet hurry is all i do

to work
to pick up the kids
to finish a design

we hurry like bees
like wine from a glass
in and out

we "brisk walk"
find time we don't have
skip a meal

when do i not hurry?

i'll make time
to hurry

i'll hurry for you

if you pick up sand
slowly release it
over days
over weeks
over years

you'll still be left
with granulated pieces

they form the growth
that is needed

the memories
that will guide you

they help you
avoid the left path
so you find the right

doing things differently

the place i belong

i'm hiding amongst
the broken sea shells and seaweed
unafraid of the tiny smooth rocks
that surround and serve to protect me

the sun slowly rises
spreading its colour

sand fleas come out to feast
before the sun takes them

the waves fall into themselves
like a meditation app
playing in the background

unpierced from within
the skin of the water lays flat
with slow sways

everyone that passes
makes an effort to see me
to them
i am someone
i am seen

even dogs seem to care
with their balls and sticks
as they sniff and brush by

the tiny waves i walk over and through
crash and run up the beach
forming white bubbles
that fizz away like lemonade

as the overcast grey
sets a gradient over the water
i no longer find a place to hide
as this is the place i belong

your best self

you've achieved a lot
what you do is impressive
you have kids, a career, a past
your own difficulties
life events and hardships

no one is alike
no one will ever compare
so don't strive to be better
through comparison
strive to be your best self
let that be your motivation
to achieve and grow

you are loved

you are loved
the most

two parts of an equal
we hold you close

you are the stars
to our night

you hold us together
keeping us bright

you are the warmth
we share

pausing time
when you're not there

you are the beauty
that fills our hearts

memories and moments
of life's precious parts

the start, the middle
where do we begin?

you are our summer
after spring

we hold you close
now and forever

both in our arms
cherished together

a graceful shift
into the unknown
sometimes reveals
the treasures at the end of a rainbow
or at the peak of a mountain

we must go beyond the seas
or through the forest sometimes
find these places of growth
of resilience
and of courage

we will find that
although our journey may be vast
it will all be worth it in the end

so that we may find
what we wish to hold so close
when we finally get there

outside comfort

growth

you search for a beginning
contemplate the middle
and master the end

only to find yourself
back at the beginning again

about the author

i was born in melbourne australia in september 1983. i'm the 3rd oldest of 8 siblings.

i enjoy running, writing, design and nutrition. i have a growth mindset where i'm always aiming to be the best version of myself. my long term goals revolve around health and wellness both physically and mentally.

i have two beautiful daughters. they are my life.

www.leemawdsley.com.au

instagram: holdthecork   **facebook:** holdthecork

www.ingramcontent.com/pod-product-compliance
Lightning Source LLC
Chambersburg PA
CBHW061749070526
44585CB00025B/2842